30 Years of Bus De

By Paul Spelzini

A Red Eagle dart seen at Hemel Hempstead

An overview of events since bus deregulation on 26th October 1986 and how it has shaped UK bus services since, with specific reference to London and the Home Counties. It also shows trends and how bus services are likely to develop in the future.

Written and compiled by Paul Spelzini c/o the Potters Bar and St. Albans Transport User Group.

Contents;

1. The preparations for deregulation.

The Transport Act 1985 was the legislation introduced under the then Conservative government led by Margaret Thatcher. This was the prelude to the deregulation of bus services outside of Greater London.

This legislation was introduced with new legislation to also deregulate the city of London, and led to the widespread introduction of electronic trading, which previously had not been used.

Prior to deregulation, bus services has been highly regulated, and operated inside London by the nationalised London Buses via London Transport and later London Regional Transport, and outside London by the National Bus Company, synonymous with their Leyland National buses which were widely used in the early 1980s throughout the UK.

A Leyland National at St. Albans Abbey railway station on a 361 service.

Prior to the introduction of deregulation, all bus operators had to register which services they wished to operate on a commercial basis, originally 42 days prior to introduction or alteration. This has since been extended to 56 days under the Transport Act 2000 et al. to allow local authorities time to decide whether to tender replacement services where commercial services have been withdrawn or reduced.

Prior to the deregulation event, many operators registered their main commercial services. However what was interesting was that they also took the opportunity to register some additional services to cover situations where tenders may have been lost, resulting in a reduction of services or garage and operation closures, which sadly did occur in some places.

However Deregulation did introduce some fascinating new concepts into public bus transport, such as the minibus revolution which occurred, where a number of services were either converted to minibus or taxi-bus; or new minibus services.

These were introduced to replace conventional service altogether, which happened also in London on some busy inner London routes such as route 28 (although later converted back to conventional double deck vehicles.

Whole new bus networks were introduced such as the Welwyn Hatfield line of bespoke Optare minibuses in a smart livery running a network of 6no. Half hourly services in Welwyn Hatfield which were a great success at the time. These featured comfortable seating and piped 'muzak' - a great change from the basic Leyland Nationals operating previously.

London Buses also took the opportunity to introduce some new routes in competition with the National Bus Company routes outside London.

These included a new 303 hourly bus from Potters Bar to Hitchin, as insurance against losing the 84 service, which was tendered as a half hourly service diverted via Potters Bar and replacing much of the old London Country North East 313 and Green Line 714 services to St. Albans and the old 884 thrice daily shopper service.

In Hertfordshire, LT route 292 was registered to Stirling corner on Sundays, and the 107 and 217 tendered also. The 317 was withdrawn between Upshire and Waltham Cross. The high frequency142 and 258 routes were tendered though.

In Surrey the 216 and 290 services were registered, but the former 215 service was tendered and the 218 to Staines was taken over by London Country as the 427. London Buses did run a half hourly 306 weekday service from Kingston though to Epsom.

In Kent, there was relatively little change apart from new services to the Bluewater shopping centre outside Dartford coming on-stream.

The rambling 242 service formerly South Mimms to Chingford was broken up into 3 sections and tendered: A half hourly Potters Bar to Waltham Abbey service; a school service from Waltham Cross to Chingford and a new LRT minibus route 367 from Chingford to the London Boundary estate. The Potters Bar to South Mimms section was replaced by the diverted 84.

There was to be a new hourly 310a weekday service from Enfield to Hertford, and revamped London Country 310/310a/311 services which streamlined a collection of old occasional loss making London Country services into a modern frequent corridor of services.

Green Line meanwhile operated a network of express coach services across London into the Home Counties. They were forced to reassess demand and a period of consolidation occurred resulting in fewer, and shorter and faster coach services.

An old BL on the 242 service which ran from Chingford-South Mimms briefly seen at Potters Bar

Throughout the rest of the UK, the talk was of the switch to smaller mini-buses with ageing larger buses switched to busier routes or replaced altogether.

In London which was still regulated; there was a tendering regime to tender loss making services. This resulted in a number of new operators taking over less popular routes, and some consolidation of busier routes. It was Centre West's novel small minibuses that caught the eye though in London, and led to minibus area schemes centred on Orpington, Barnet, Uxbridge, Kingston and Greenford.

An MB seen at Potters Bar on the 313, a route that now runs within London but used to run out to Whipsnade Zoo in Bedfordshire before 1986.

2. Events after deregulation in the late 1980s.

The period after deregulation led to many changes, not least the public getting used to new bus networks throughout the UK, and around London and the Home Counties particularly.

New unfamiliar services appeared literally overnight, and routes that had been in existence since the 1930's in many cases, either changed significantly or disappeared overnight in response to deregulation. However new services appeared to take their place in many cases, although some casualties did occur.

The saddest casualty arguably was the tendering of London Buses then Loughton bus garage's routes. London Buses managed to lose all of their routes, here resulting in the closure of the garage that had functioned since the early 20th century. The routes were taken over by Grey Green and other private companies in many cases, later to become Arriva.

Deregulation also led to the wide use of minibuses which were successfully introduced on many routes, to either keep them commercial or replace loss making former routes.

One of the most successful and eye catching networks introduced from scratch was the Welwyn Hatfield Line in central Hertfordshire. This introduced small luxurious Optare minibuses running half hourly six days a week across the new towns, and largely replacing a network of old occasional and failing London Country North East routes, such as the 340 and 340b.

The old 350 and 350a routes south of Hertford to Barnet were also withdrawn leaving parts of Hertfordshire with no regular bus service.

Welwyn Hatfield Line service W5 in Welwyn Garden City, summer 1987.

However representations by User Groups such as ours, resulted in some new services being introduced in this period to plug some gaps left by deregulation.

This led to new services to places like Hadley Wood with the 399 and Crews Hill with the W10, now both since taken over by Transport for London. Both these areas previously had only rail stations.

Conversely the rail station and small hamlet at Bayford, 2 stops further north of Crews Hill now only gets a 308/380 Centrebus service several days a week now.

London Buses did introduce a 310b variant on Saturdays just before 1990, and these routes ran until around 2002 when they were both withdrawn.

In the country at large, the process of privatising the bus companies began, with London Country split into North East, North West, South East and South West; all later to be reunited as Arriva with Grey Green.

Competition did spring up on many busy routes, but tended to die out after about 6 months due to changing usage patterns. Sustaining competition was draining on the major commercial operators, who tend not to compete head to head these days as it tends to hit profit margins.

Most competition was either in the tendering process, which allowed controlled change; or between the big five groups (Arriva, Stagecoach, Abellio, First and RATP groups) and smaller local operators.

An older style Alexander VRM double deck bus used at deregulation displaying Herts contract service board from the late 1980s.

3. The 1990s and how services responded

The 1990s saw the privatisation of the big nationalised bus company subsidiaries, broken up for sale to the main groups, which still exist today in their various forms.

London Country North East became part of the Sovereign group based in Yorkshire, but later sold off property assets such as high value garages for development, especially in the South East but lost many services through tendering.

Many former National bus company groups were bought up and later amalgamated into the Arriva group, which still control many of their former subsidiaries.

Arriva also bought up Grey Green coaches in London, and several of the new London bus companies.

London Buses was broken up into companies covering geographical slices from the centre out to the London boundary, and sold to the highest bidders.

Many were snapped up by the main groups; such as Arriva, Go Ahead, Abellio, RATP First and others.

One or two remained independent such as Metroline, later buying up London Northern and First West London operations following a Monopolies and Merger Commission investigation; as First group also operated the parallel Great Western Rail Franchise.

A similar operation occurred in Scotland with City link as First Group also won the Scot rail franchise.

A London Buses 310A seen at Waltham Cross in 1990. Lea Valley also ran their own version of this service until its demise around 2000.

Following competition around the country after deregulation, service patterns settled down into a more routine pattern after a spate of rapid changes.

This led to an acknowledgement by operators that it may be possible to share some routes rather than compete for the whole service on the busier routes. This had advantages in that it gave the impression of a frequent service whilst only providing a proportion of the costs and risk.

Economics also had a part to play, with declining patronage leading to rising fares and costs, around 1990 onwards when inflation was high and people simply couldn't afford high fares or cut back on travel. The private car was also growing in popularity, and bus use nationally was now in decline.

Operators also noticed that where competition was concerned, a one man bus carrying 72 passengers was more profitable than a minibus carrying 23 people maximum.

The attractiveness of the minibus started to fade, and by 2000 many of the bus subsidiaries and London Buses had already been sold off to the major groups.

The larger groupings also started to buy out small operators such as the excellent Welwyn Hatfield line, replacing them with conventional single decker buses, which was seen as backward step by some.

Arriva also bought some key routes from rival operators, such as the central 300/301 through central Hertfordshire from Sovereign, who later sold off their remaining Hertfordshire operations.

Arriva's 300/301 'Central line' route through Herts seen in St. Albans with a Metroline 84. These routes changed ownership several times during the 1990s from National Bus to Sovereign then Arriva.

By the late 1990s, economic reality had set in, and many of the routes introduced at deregulation were being consolidated or rationalised. A number were withdrawn and condensed into streamlined services. This was mainly in response to the major groups having acquired the National bus company subsidiaries and eliminating duplication between services to maximise profit.

This also led to a reduction in the number of services being operated by minibuses, as the minibus revolution started to fade. Newer single deckers being gradually being introduced to replace them, notably the Wright bodied Dart which became the mainstay for many routes, even today.

4. The Decade 2000–2010

The first decade of the 21st Century saw further consolidation of the major bus groups, resulting in takeovers and regrouping and rebranding of some operators.

This was very much the case in London. With the emergence of Arriva, First and Stagecoach and Go Ahead subsidiaries close to their current forms.

Further buyouts occurred with Metroline becoming part of the Delgro-Comfort international transport group. It seemed that size mattered in the new deregulated marketplace.

The early part of this decade was fairly quiet, with relatively few changes in service types or developments, as most operators concentrated on consolidating their networks and making them profitable.

The big change in this decade was the growth of school bus services that went from one or two services to whole networks in a short space of time, as demand exploded with growing school place demand and limited existing transport.

Changes in legislation also helped as Euro standards introduced for emissions control and accessibility requirements, meant that private transport may no longer comply, so was often put out to tender by the education and transport authorities.

This resulted in the TFL dial a ride and accessibility bus networks, provided in addition to public services.

Outside London, school services boomed and this added to traffic congestion which started to become a more serious problem for operators.

Low floor buses also started to be introduced as part of the Disabled Discrimination Act, so the high floor minibuses which had held sway since deregulation were gradually replaced by Darts in most cases.

A low floor Dart seen in St. Albans, common throughout the UK since 2002.

The latter part of this decade saw some new types of services being introduced, as part of new low cost subsidiaries mainly intended to win tenders.

In Watford, several Shopper routes were introduced by Metroline, the 318 and 346, later taken over by Mullaneys, a private company who adopted a similar livery, but now operate a large network of 22 school routes as well as regular hire coaches.

2007 saw the redevelopment of the Herts University site in Hatfield and start-up of UNO buses, using section 106 funding. This has proved to be a good source of funding for local authorities through the planning system to develop new bus services, but has a limited lifespan.

This can lead to rapid growth of new services, but equally can lead to their rapid demise when the money runs out. This could happen in 2018 in Welwyn Hatfield.

The rise and rise of private school buses; PPH modern double deckers often seen in St. Albans.

New operators often use their own numbering and control systems. This has led to problems with the likes of UNO using a separate numbering system that contradicts the established route numbering order, causing confusion amongst passengers. This has often been a cause for public complaint.

They also use vehicles that are ill suited to established routes, for instance introducing wide bodied Citaro's more suited to an airport than narrow historic streets like St. Albans, Canterbury or York. This was one reason the Mercedes Citaro 'bendy buses' were withdrawn in central London due to rising cyclist casualties.

'Your bus' Mercedes Citaro Y3 seen in Derby. Wide bodied buses were introduced for modern towns, but are not ideal for narrow potholed streets in historic city centres.

The latter part of this decade also saw a sharp rise in airport growth, up to 22% in the case of Stansted, with Heathrow and Gatwick now approaching capacity. Bus and coach services to airports also grew in this decade, although some have faltered, due to changes in flight patterns and demand.

This occurred mainly when EasyJet and also later Ryanair relocated a number of flights to Southend and Europe in late 2000s. A number of services to Stansted had to be deregistered as a result, mainly serving East Anglia.

The other main event in this decade was the recession in the UK, and bailing out the banks. This lead to a slump in demand, resulting in some works bus services disappearing particularly.

The growth in airport services is relentless. National Express coach seen at Stansted, 2015.

5. 2010 to the present day.

Since the recession, business has slowly recovered resulting in slow growth of the economy and bus and coach services with it. However there has also been a rise in costs as a result with higher taxes, mainly VAT and other costs.

The growth in school services has been relentless, with some schools now using both public and private bus networks simply to cope with demand and growth. Expansion has seen new operators sucked in and a whole variety of vehicles used dating from 2000 upwards.

A new development has been the rise of the taxi-bus, now widely used for private schools and some colleges. This has been very popular as it is small enough to fit down small roads and flexible enough to cater for 1-12 people. It can also be driven 'without hire or reward' by non-PCV registered drivers, and these services don't need to be registered normally, which makes these very popular with schools, charities and smaller operators.

Mercedes Minibuses, now widely used by private schools

The main change that has occurred this decade so far is the public funding cuts. This occurred first of all round 2011, when a number of services were trimmed back, resulting in some reductions to low usage services and heavy loss makers.

Since then further cuts have progressed resulting in more serious cuts affecting many evening and weekend bus services right across the country. Fares have also started to rise in real terms for the first time in some years.

Up until now. Transport for London has been exempt from this, but even now there are reductions to many outer suburban services that are lightly used, with some reductions on retendering starting to gather pace.

Many operators are using older vehicles due to cost cutting measures, with fewer new vehicles being introduced than before. The Local Transport Sustainability fund has resulted in some new vehicles and funding for GPS ticket machines and promotion mainly. However the cost of handling cash fares is a real problem now with many banks using mechanised money handling systems to reduce costs.

This has resulted in both an explosion in smartcard development, and mobile phones being used for tickets on buses and coaches.

National Express now use systems where you can print tickets at home also, although the coach network has shrunk in the UK recently.

Discount cards are also becoming more widely used to promote low cost affordable bus travel for students mainly.

Public advert for mobile phone ticketing now commonly used outside London.

The current period is seeing a period of consolidation of services, although not much change is expected to the basic network at the present time as usage patterns are fairly stable. However the proposed Brexit negotiations could see companies and people exiting the UK, resulting in a number of potential changes.

Another change is low cost operators coming into towards London from the coastal counties and South Midlands tendering for public services at very low rates.

They are winning more and more services but ultimately, this is at the risk of very high dead mileage and the risk of rising fuel prices, and could go bust on low cost fixed price tenders with no allowances for rising prices.

We have already seen this with the likes of Jubilee Coaches and Seamarks remote operations in the past since deregulation, resulting in emergency tenders and disruption to services.

New Regional operators have sprung up taking over traditional contracts. This is Redline on the S4 in St. Albans on the high frequency S4/5 contract offering Wi-Fi.

6. The future for bus and coach travel

So what does the future hold for bus and coach travel in the world, UK and Hertfordshire?

One clue may be to look at what is already happening in Europe and the USA, as they tend to be about 10 years ahead of the UK in terms of transport investment.

In Europe the Microbus is well established and has been since 2008. The Breda 10 seat electric Microbus already operates widely in Italy. In France the Gruau 10 seat Microbus is now in use along the coastal towns and cities and proving popular.

There seems to be a rationale here. Provincial towns such as Biarritz have circa 5 commercial single deck frequent bus routes, and 2 tourism budget funded Microbus routes serving the beach and coastal part of the resort.

There are no longer occasional services apart from longer distance coaches. Other journeys are now by taxi or ambulance. Perhaps the UK can learn from that.

Another interesting development is that most western cities of the USA and Canada including Vancouver have reintroduced modern single deck trolleybuses on main routes.

Articulated or bendy buses also roam the streets of Seattle and San Francisco which have wide streets.

In Portland, Oregon, they have gone much further with modern trams, a cable car to the hospital located on a hill and a pedestrian and tram only cable stayed bridge.

The Gruau Microbus has proved very popular in France, and is versatile and often operates fully loaded, mainly with senior citizens.

Its funding through the tourism network is interesting, showing that different services are provided by different agencies and for different purposes, unlike the UK.

Its main advantage is to provide a frequent service to areas where bus use is low, with minimal funding and to provide a regular service to improve accessibility.

Gruau 10 seat electric Microbus on tourism funded free coastal service in Biarritz, September 2014.

The future for bus services in the UK and elsewhere may rely on funding through advertising revenues.

This concept is currently being trialled in the USA and if successful, could be introduced in the UK using vinyl folding TV screens with real time displays. This would allow live streaming of TV programmes on the sides of vehicles.

Buses would in effect become mobile advertising platforms, replacing the mobile advertising vehicles we currently see.

We could therefore see both public and private bus networks, and private networks may have to be 'opened up' for public use, but that may take a change in legislation via the Buses Bill and after the UK leaves the European Economic Union.

The 'Willie bus' concept of all over advertising and scrolling route information with street maps on trial currently in the USA

Another concept shown at the Geneva motor show in 2013 was the excellent Rinspeed Micromax electric bus.

This is currently being considered by Volkswagen for mass production, and could be available from approximately Euro15, 000 in theory.

This bus would have a bike rack at the back, and be small enough to use bus lanes, but also narrow streets and off street locations.

The idea is to trial this privately for pre-booked or VIP bus use, and similar to 'dial a ride' before considering low usage routes for public service.

However it is the Breda Microbus that has been a proven success in Europe, and now Mellow in the UK are developing a similar electric bus for right hand drive use in the UK.

Interior of the Orion E, the first new all electric Microbus designed for UK use.

The BYD all electric double decker London bus seen on route 98

About the Author;

Paul was 59 at the time of writing this book, and married over 30 years with 3 children, and a grand-daughter; plus an Old English sheepdog puppy called Bella. Paul is a Chartered Surveyor and Engineer by training, with over 40 years' experience.

He is also a voluntary station adopter with the Abbey Line Community rail partnership since its inception in 2005; and has run a voluntary local transport user group since 1986.

He is also a leading UK flight and traditional archer.

Paul has written a number of published and self-published books plus some published articles; including 'My Wonderful Fran', 'Artificial Nocturne', '30 years of bus deregulation' and 'Planning and Development; changing the way we travel.'

All available now on Amazon.

*If you enjoyed reading this book, then perhaps you may enjoy reading other books by the same author;

'My Wonderful Fran', 'Artificial Nocturne' and 'Planning and Development; changing the way we travel', are now also available on Amazon Kindle.

Thank you for reading this compilation.

amazon